YOU CAN BE A WOMAN OCEANOGRAPHER

Sharon Roth Franks
and
Judith Love Cohen

Illustrations:
David A. Katz

Editing:
Janice J. Martin

Cascade
Pass, Inc.

First Edition 1994
You Can Be a Woman Oceanographer was written by Sharon Roth Franks and Judith Love Cohen, designed and illustrated by David Katz, and edited by Janice Martin.

This book is one of a series that emphasizes the value of science and mathematical studies by depicting real women whose careers provide inspirational role models. Other books in the series include:
You Can Be A Woman Engineer
You Can Be A Woman Architect
You Can Be A Woman Marine Biologist
You Can Be A Woman Zoologist
You Can Be A Woman Egyptologist
You Can Be A Woman Paleontologist

Library of Congress Cataloging-in-Publication Data
Franks, Sharon Roth, 1961-
      You can be a woman oceanographer / Sharon Roth Franks and Judith Love
Cohen ; illustrations, David A. Katz ; editing, Janice J. Martin. -- 1st ed.
         p.   cm.
    ISBN 1-880599-14-7 : $6.00
     1. Oceanography--Vocational guidance--Juvenile literature. 2. Vocational guidance
for women--Juvenile literature. [1. Oceanography. 2. Occupations.]   I. Cohen, Judith
Love, 1933-   . II. Katz, David A. (David Arthur), 1949-   ill. III. Martin, Janice J.
IV. Title.
GC30.5.F73   1994   94-14982
551.46'.0023--dc20   CIP

Dedication

This book is dedicated by author Sharon Franks to Dr. Peter John Selwyn Franks, a first-rate oceanographer who is still a kid at heart.

This book is also dedicated by illustrator David Katz to his brother, Jack, who always loved the ocean and took inspiration from it every day.

The deck of the ship is covered with various metallic things like A-frames, winches, and cables; and a few deliberately nonmetallic things like big fiberglass cones for trapping particles. Hanging from a large A-frame is a small submarine (called a "submersible"). Sharon steps carefully around the cables and ducks her head under the vehicle called "Alvin."

Sharon copies the serial numbers of some of the instruments in her log book while the crewman with her checks that the equipment is securely tied down.

"Would you like to go inside?" he asks, pointing to Alvin. He helps her climb up the ladder and into the hatch on top of the little vehicle. As she sits inside, Sharon closes her eyes.

Sharon Franks is with a team of oceanographers above the Juan de Fuca Ridge in the northeast Pacific Ocean. Two of the scientists are going down to the undersea ridge of mountains, 2200 meters below the surface of the ocean.

Sharon imagines what they will see! In her mind she sees huge, rocky chimneys, 30 meters tall. She imagines the hot jets of liquid spewing out of these chimneys, and instead of swimming away from what looks like an erupting underwater volcano, dozens of small light-reflective animals (clams, crabs, tube worms) are basking in the nourishing flow.

Soon they will be on station, and the scientists will go down to look for the best places to deploy the moorings. Each mooring assembly consists of instruments, an anchor and some floats. The instruments will provide important information about these hot jets of liquid. The instruments will remain in place for one year, and are then retrieved.

Going to sea is wonderful, but going underneath the sea is Sharon's dream.

But how did Dr. Sharon Roth Franks get here? Why is she doing this? Let her tell us her story, the story of a geological oceanographer . . .

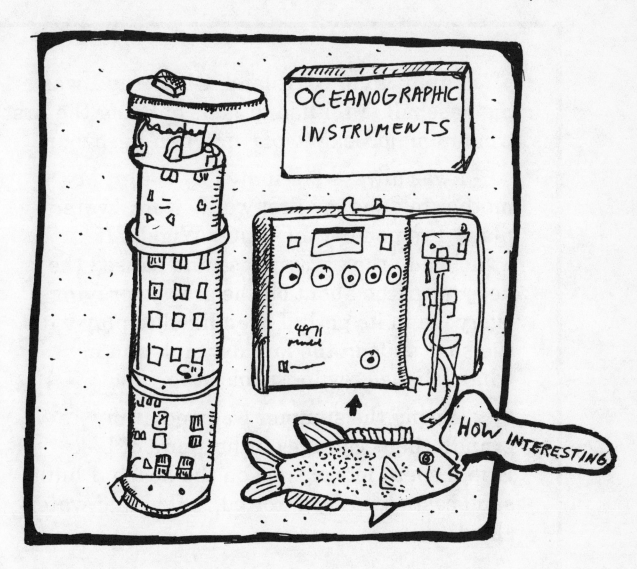

I grew up in Cleveland, Ohio, and I was a big baseball fan. I had dreams of being the first woman major league player when I grew up.

I was always fascinated by water. My mother told me my first words were "water play." I remember my Water Wiggle. It attached to the garden hose and caused the hose to writhe about on the grass, spraying everyone in its path. I even liked to play with the soap suds in the laundry sink and my whale-shaped toy in the bathtub.

During the summer we lived at my grandfather's cottage on the shore of Lake Erie. I spent lots of time on the beach. I built sand castles, canoed, rowed, sailed and water-skied.

When I was ten I was interested in almost everything: math, science, swimming, ice skating, animals of all kinds . . . and lunch!

Later, I focused more on nature. In high school I had a class called Nature Study. The teacher often took us out of the classroom, and we studied trees, wildflowers and birds. I knew I wanted to spend my life dealing with science and nature in some way, but I wasn't sure exactly what way that might be.

I went to college at Dartmouth in New Hampshire. In the beginning, I studied the Russian language, and then on a whim I enrolled in a geology class. I wasn't sure what the difference was between geology and geography, nor did I know that all rocks were not just "rocks."

I learned about volcanoes, mountains, crystals, fossils and ore deposits, and about how the Earth changes. I learned about how new ocean crust is created near the undersea volcanoes, and how the crust is destroyed when it slides beneath another piece of the Earth's crust (like the end of an escalator). I decided to major in Earth Sciences so I could study more about these things.

One day a geophysicist came to present a seminar on deep-sea hydrothermal vents. The vents are like hot springs or geysers on the ocean floor. I don't remember breathing or moving. I just sat there in a trance. I wanted to study deep sea venting!

After graduation I went to work for the professor who gave the talk. My first research cruise lasted three weeks, and I was soon hooked on going to sea. Later, I went to graduate school and studied oceanography with a focus on marine geology. But oceanography is much more complicated than any search for underwater vents!

UNDER WATER
VOLCANO

Oceanography is the study of the oceans, but since that covers so much information, the subject is usually divided into four parts:

1. Biological Oceanography covers the study of plants and animals that live in the ocean and how they interact with their environment.

2. Chemical Oceanography is the study of the composition of sea water and how it changes when other substances dissolve in it or settle out of it.

3. Physical Oceanography covers the movements of water in the ocean. Waves are a kind of movement you can see on the surface. Other movements include tides and currents. The wind and changes in the temperature and saltiness of sea water produce the movements.

4. Geological Oceanography is the study of the rocks and sediment on the seafloor. It also includes the study of undersea volcanoes and earthquakes which are related to movement of the ocean crust.

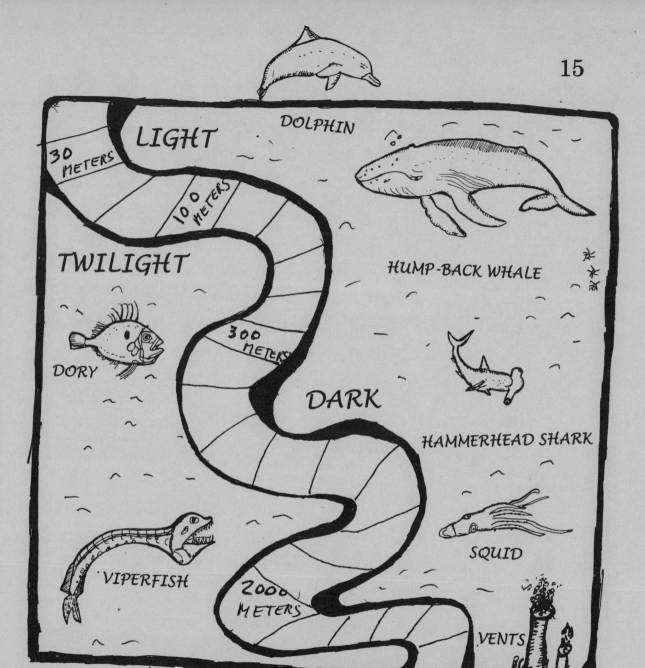

THE OCEAN ENVIRONMENT CHANGES AS YOU GO DEEPER

Marine geology (geological oceanography) was my field. I was most fascinated by the study of seafloor movement. Geologists discovered that the ocean crust is constantly, slowly changing. Along seafloor spreading ridges, hot, molten rock flows upward from the inside of the Earth and hardens to form new ocean crust. As new crust is produced, older crust is pushed outward, away from the ridge. New crust is produced at about the same rate that a fingernail grows. Ocean crust is destroyed at the same rate it is produced, so the surface area of the Earth stays the same.

"Plate tectonics" is the theory that explains movement of the Earth's crust. This crust is broken into a dozen or so large plates, like the cracked shell of a hard-boiled egg. When two plates collide, it is common to find mountains or volcanoes. The first clue scientists had that the plates were moving was that the east coast of North and South America seems to fit like pieces of a jigsaw puzzle with the west coast of Europe and Africa. They wondered if the continents had once been joined and later broke apart.

17

Now that I knew what marine geology was, I had to learn how to do it. Fortunately, I had a chance to do research projects.

The deep sea hot springs (vents) are found where new ocean crust forms - along seafloor spreading centers. Near the hot springs are communities of remarkable animals that are able to survive with the great pressures of the deep sea and without the usual sources of plant food that come from the sunlit upper layers of the ocean.

It is important to study what comes out of these vents and where it goes. You need to know this whether you are primarily interested in geology and want to know how the ocean floor is changing, or whether you are more interested in the gases and chemicals added to the oceans. Perhaps you are most interested in the new kinds of food supplies that do not need sunlight, but instead use the chemicals in the hot springs.

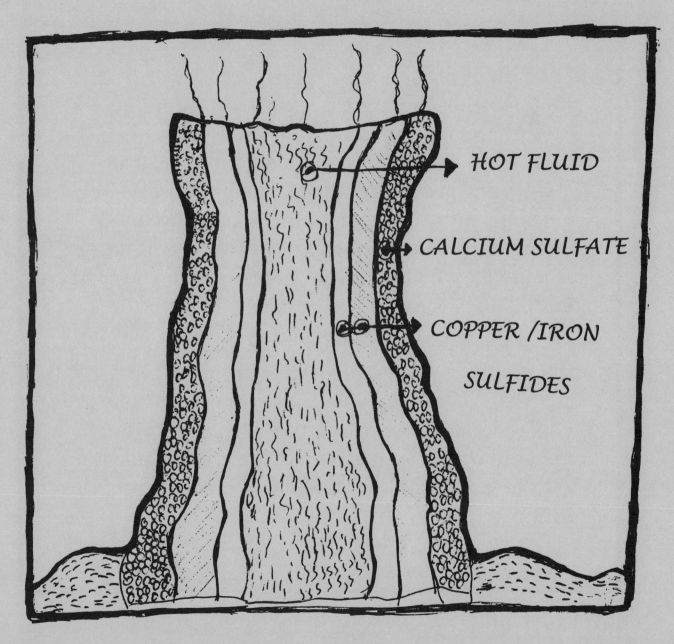

HOT FLUID

CALCIUM SULFATE

COPPER /IRON

SULFIDES

You're probably familiar with photosynthesis. Green plants grow by using sunlight as energy. Down in the depths of the ocean, the sunlight never penetrates. Instead, something called chemosynthesis occurs. Without any sunlight, bacteria grow by using chemical energy from the hot springs and later become food for the larger creatures in the food chain.

My research involved measuring the amount of particles like copper and carbon in the water at various depths around the hot water vents. In scientific research, it is often very important to measure things carefully, and to take lots of measurements to make sure your data is sufficient.

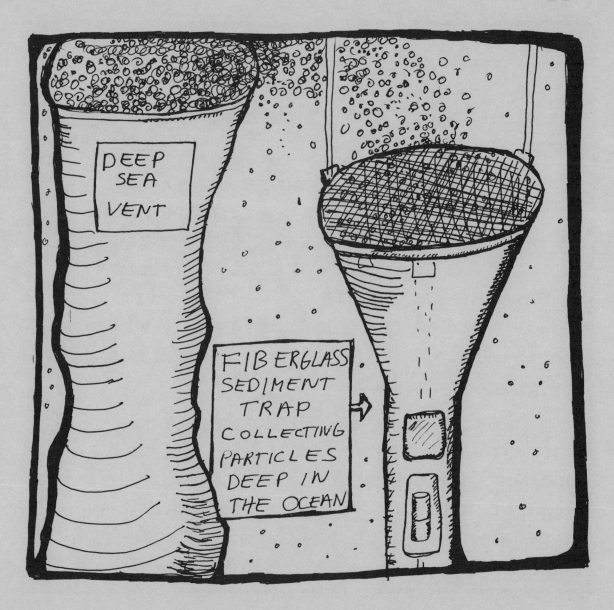

We used sediment traps to collect the solid particles that come out of the hot water vents. They resemble 8-foot-tall fiberglass ice cream cones.

These traps, tied to moorings, were put in place from a large ship (a research vessel) and left in place for a year. When the time came to retrieve the traps, we sent a sound signal to unhook the anchors. Then the traps, which had floats attached, came up to the surface where we could see them and bring them back on board the ship.

We then had the job of measuring and analyzing the particles in each trap at each location and at each depth. We expected that there would be a gradual change in the amount of each type of particle as the depth and distance from the vent increased.

Our conclusions showed that the products of chemosynthesis, called organic carbon particles, are carried by currents away from the vents. As they move through the water, the particles settle gradually, but unevenly. At some depths organic carbon particles are mysteriously missing. We think that hungry creatures that live in the deep sea eat some of these particles. But there may be other explanations for this mystery, and scientists should not jump to conclusions.

Today, I am studying Earth's atmosphere as well as its oceans. I am helping teachers and students understand global climate change. Throughout history the Earth has changed. There have been ice ages and warmer periods, but the major changes happened slowly. Now, humans may be changing the environment so fast that they will change the global climate.

20,000 B.C.: "TODAY'S WEATHER FOR THE NEXT 1000 YEARS ---FREEZING, FREEZING, FREEZING!"
TINY ICEBERGS
ICE
ICE
ICEBERGS
MORE ICEBERGS
IT'S TOO COLD!
ICE
ICE
ICE
SMALL ICEBERGS

How can you tell if you would be good at oceanography? If you can answer yes to the following questions, then you should consider becoming an oceanographer.

1. Are you inquisitive? Do you like to think about how things work and why?

Oceanographers have a multitude of mysteries to solve. There are many processes you can study. You can examine the connections between plants and animals in a food web. You can understand how the oceans are mixed and how that affects climate, or you can probe the mysteries of the driving force behind plate tectonics. Someone who wants to know why and how things happen will find plenty of unanswered questions to capture her interest.

2. Do you like to be out in nature?

While some oceanographers use computers and never go to sea, I love to go out on the ocean. Being part of a team on board a ship is fun. Here, you can truly experience the power and size of the ocean in a way that is impossible to do on land.

3. Do you like to think three-dimensionally and portray your information visually?

It is not enough for ocean scientists to do their experiments. They must share their findings with other scientists and the public. To make what they have to say easier to understand, all scientists use drawings and graphs and other visual aids. Ocean tides, currents, winds, etc., influence the whole globe, and it is particularly important for oceanographers to describe their work visually.

Today oceanographers use unmanned and robotic vehicles and instruments to do much of their work, just like space engineers who rely on satellites for information instead of manned space travel. Although my early dream of diving in a submersible has not happened, I have found many different challenges.

What I like best about my career as an oceanographer is that I have many subjects to think about. I am learning how the processes that happen in the ocean are connected to what is happening on land and in the air. I am concerned about teaching others how to understand these connections. We must all know that environmental changes that begin in one area may affect other areas as well. We can make better decisions to keep our planet healthy if we understand this.

When I look ahead, I would like to do more to bridge the gap between what scientists are finding and what the general public understands.

Most scientists conduct research on very focused subjects, and they often write about their findings in language that is not easily understood by nonspecialists. In order for all of us to make wise decisions about the care of our planet, it is important that scientists and nonscientists alike understand the implications of scientific results.

I have chosen to be an interpreter, translating the language of science to a language understood by everyone. I plan to do much more of this in the future.

In order to be an oceanographer, you need to be curious about how the ocean works. You can study grains of sand on the shore, sea life far off shore, the motion of the waves, volcanoes along spreading ridges, or how plants use nutrients dissolved in sea water to grow. You can even work to design the clever instruments used to study many of these things.

If you want to go out and see things for yourself, like luminous clam shells a mile under the ocean's surface; if you want to understand why the ocean temperature changes and relate these findings with charts and pictures; if you are interested in how our future oceans are evolving from the distant past, then you can do it too. You can be a woman oceanographer.

YOU CAN BE A WOMAN OCEANOGRAPHER
SCIENCE LESSON PLAN 1

PURPOSE: To gain an understanding of how oceanographers collect organisms from the deep sea and to demonstrate how the choice of equipment determines what they learn.

MATERIALS: Water-filled tank, assorted objects (beads, plastic sea life), two nets of different mesh sizes, shallow plastic container. The objects range in size from smaller than the opening in the small mesh to larger than those in the large mesh.

PROCEDURES: Add objects to water-filled tank. Stir the tank just before each child takes a turn.

Give the first child the larger mesh net. Have the child close his eyes since it is too dark to see deep beneath the surface of the ocean. Have the child sweep net once through tank.

Next, help child empty "catch" into plastic container. Discuss collection.

Repeat, with another child and the other size mesh net.

CONCLUSIONS: Were there differences in the collections when different nets were used?

Were there differences when the net was swept at different depths?

What differences would you expect if the plastic fish could swim away?

SCIENCE LESSON PLAN 2

PURPOSE: To gain a familiarity with oceanographic instrument moorings and how they are anchored and recovered.

MATERIALS: Water-filled tank, balloons (slightly blown-up), paper clips (half opened), string, colored pipe cleaners, whistle, metal washers.

PROCEDURES: Have children assemble instrument moorings as follows: Tie a length of string, which represents the mooring line, onto the balloon (the balloon represents the float). Make sure the string is shorter than the depth of the water in the tank. Add a bent paper clip to the other end of the string (mooring line). The paper clip represents the release mechanism. Add three instruments to the mooring (three pipe cleaners of different color).

Have the children deploy the moorings by taking them to a spot in the tank and releasing the balloon end of the string, holding on to the paper clip (release end). The metal washers represent the anchors. Fasten them to the release mechanism and let them sink.

To recover the moorings, have one child blow a whistle. In the real world this would trigger a release of the anchor. Have a child unhook the paper clip. The float will rise to the surface.

CONCLUSIONS: What is the purpose of the float, the anchor and the release?

Why would you want to leave the instruments untended?

Do scientists really use balloons in the ocean? (No. Strong glass spheres are used instead.)

SCIENCE LESSON PLAN 3

PURPOSE: To determine the different life forms that live at different ocean depths.

MATERIALS: Posterboard, drawing materials (crayons, colored pens, paper), variety of books with pictures of sea life, scissors, glue.

PROCEDURES: Have the children divide the posterboard into different depths: 100 meters, 500 meters, 1000 meters, etc.

Have the children draw or cut out pictures of sea animals or plants appropriate to each level of the ocean depth and glue them onto the posterboard at the appropriate depth.

CONCLUSIONS: What kinds of plants and animals are found closest to the surface?

What are the animals and plants like in the deepest regions?

How do they differ?

RESOURCES: Library books on ocean life such as *Exploring the Sea, Oceanography Today.*

About the Authors:

Dr. Sharon E. Roth Franks is now an oceanographer in the Education Department of the Stephen Birch Aquarium-Museum at the Scripps Institution of Oceanography in San Diego. Prior to this, she received her doctorate in geological oceanography from Oregon State University and her bachelor's degree from Dartmouth College in New Hampshire. Dr. Franks' research has focused on deep-sea particle plumes emanating from hydrothermal vents in the northeast Pacific Ocean. She has participated in numerous research cruises, many of which have been aboard Canadian research vessels. Among her nonacademic interests are bread-making and ice cream-making.

Judith Love Cohen is a Registered Professional Electrical Engineer with bachelor's and master's degrees in engineering from the University of Southern California and University of California at Los Angeles. She has written plays, screenplays, and newspaper articles in addition to her series of children's books that began with *You Can Be a Woman Engineer*.

About the Illustrator:

David Arthur Katz received his training in art education and holds a master's degree from the University of South Florida. He is a credentialed teacher in the Los Angeles Unified School District. His involvement in the arts has included animation, illustration, and play-, poetry- and song-writing.